# The Gospel According to Waffle House

## Reimagining the Community of Faith

### RONNIE McBRAYER

THE GOSPEL ACCORDING TO WAFFLE HOUSE

ISBN-10: 061592025X
ISBN-13: 978-0615920252 (Match Point)

# DEDICATION

For the Congregation of A Simple Faith

"These are my people. I'm a Waffle House guy. I've got to stay in touch with that." – Roy McAvoy (Kevin Costner) in *Tin Cup*

# CONTENTS

# BEFORE YOU BEGIN

In the summer of 2007 I had the opportunity to partner with a magnificent group of people, people who would form the nucleus of a most non-traditional congregation called "A Simple Faith" in Santa Rosa Beach, Florida. First meeting around a kitchen table, then spilling into the adjoining living area, and finally inhabiting storefront space, this group aimed to honor its namesake: Simplicity.

We had a core belief that following Christ together – and "doing church" – ought to be a little less complicated than our previous experiences had proven. Further, a community of faith ought to be easily accessed by those who have never really given faith a try, and those who swore they would never go to church again.

As this unique congregation began to take

shape, none of us really knew where it was going. After all, having a grand strategic plan seemed to be an obstacle to maintaining simplicity, not fostering it. More so, when something new begins, it goes and grows in directions that those who first plant the seeds can never imagine. With this in mind, I even cautioned the group: "If we take this path, the church might not become what you think it will become – so much so, that half of you won't be here in the coming years." That statistic proved true. Many of the original "Simple Faithers" moved along to other adventures; even me.

I left A Simple Faith in 2011. Obligations to extended family called me, my wife, and children away. Vocationally, I spent the next two years writing, speaking in a wide variety of church settings, and observing the religious landscape of our culture. As I wrote, spoke, and observed, I never escaped my own words, words I had written to A Simple Faith for our first "organized" meeting years before:

*"The last thing our community needs is another church; but it surely needs a place of simplicity and substance where people can learn what it means to follow Christ, worship God, love their neighbors, and serve*

*the world. That's the kind of place I want to
be a part of – that's the kind of group that I
hope we can bring together."*

Such places and groups, I'm sad to report
from my own observations, are few and far
between on America's religious landscape.
But, through a series of inexplicable events
(events that warrant their own printed pages),
my family and I returned to Santa Rosa
Beach, Florida and A Simple Faith. I am now
experiencing the rarest of happenings:
Leading the same congregation for a second
time. A reference from T.S. Elliot is
unavoidable here. He wrote:

*With the drawing of this Love and the voice
of this Calling
We shall not cease from exploration
And the end of all our exploring
Will be to arrive where we started
And know the place for the first time.**

This small book is the transcript of the
first series of sermons I delivered upon my
return to A Simple Faith. It was a way of
refocusing both the preacher and the
congregation on the "voice of this Calling" we
share. Though unorthodox, and at times

bordering on the irreverent, I entitled the five-part series of talks, "The Gospel According to Waffle House." It was, I hope, a creative attempt at repeating those things that brought the group together in the first place, but without simply repeating it. And I am happy that those who first heard this series responded enthusiastically to the meal placed before them.

Thus, I have cleaned up my sermon notes (though I have left large sections exactly as they were spoken) and formatted these words for you, the reader (though I avoided heavily editing the words in order to maintain the spirit of these talks). I hope that you can find something in these "scattered, smothered, and covered" pages – maybe just one thing – that will rekindle your faith or aid in your congregation becoming a "place of simplicity and substance where people can learn what it means to follow Christ, worship God, love their neighbors, and serve the world."

If so, then our time at this table has not been wasted.

Ronnie McBrayer
Santa Rosa Beach, Florida
Autumn, 2013

# ONE

## It's About People

When it became apparent that God and the universe were conspiring to bring my family and I back to Florida and back to A Simple Faith, I began to think about our earliest days together in 2007. Gathering around a kitchen table, the first "Faithers" loosely plotted a future, a future guided by a simple three-fold statement: "We will be a community of faith committed to worshipping God, following Christ, and serving the world." No denominationalism. No capital campaigns. No huge doctrinal treatises. No high-power marketing plans. Just a group of friends, attempting to gather for worship, follow the way of Jesus, and love our neighbors: No more, no less.

Coming back to this place, which is now for me A Simple Faith 2.0, I've been thinking a lot about how to rekindle and refocus myself – refocus us all – on that original intent. I'm not saying that we have strayed from it, but I want to make sure we never do. So my thinking has been along these lines:

How can I take us back to that original purpose, and say it again, without just saying it again?

How can I initiate a conversation about our purpose, calling, and mission as a group of people, and not just talk about it, but craft a metaphor for what it looks like?

How can I create an experiential story that we can all identify with, and a story that we can all share together?

How can I paint a picture or tell a story that will crawl into our imaginations so that we "get it."

And I intentionally say "our" and "we" because I need this too. In fact, most of the talks I give have nothing to do with telling you anything. I'm trying to figure it out for myself. You get the misfortune of eavesdropping on what's going on inside my head, a peculiar place, I assure you (and if you don't believe me, then maybe the next few weeks will verify that the thoughts in my head are indeed, quite bizarre). So, all this said, today I am beginning a series of talks about us:

Who are we?

Why are we here?

How will we fulfill our vocation as the body of Christ in this place and time?

What will we do with this little faith niche that has been given to us?

Understand, these talks will not focus on questions and answers; on foundational documents or mission statements; nor will I spend any time setting definite goals for the future or reminiscing about the past. No, instead I want to talk to you about:

> *The dietary joys of "scattered, smothered, and covered" hash browns… Working off a buzz with Cheese 'N Eggs at 3:00 AM… Alice's Ice Tea…Burt's Chili… Christmas Eve patty melts…Southern-fried waitresses… Walleyed truck drivers… Toothless fry cooks… And strong coffee…*

My series topic for the next few weeks is this: "The Gospel According to Waffle House."

This is what I have realized of late, about

A Simple Faith, and about church in general: No, we don't need more churches as we have previously known church. We don't need more straight-laced, behavior-management obsessed, bottom-line focused, boundary-drawing corporations calling themselves the body of Christ. We need these things we call churches to look more like Waffle House restaurants.

Now, I know the stereotypes and all the bad jokes:

> *What has eight arms, eight legs, and twelve teeth? The night shift at the Waffle House.*
>
> *Going to Waffle House reminds me of my father: I love watching an old man fry an egg while smoking a cigarette.*
>
> *How do you know that everyone is drunk in Waffle House? Because they have pictures of the food on the menu.*
>
> *And in Atlanta – corporate and original home of Waffle House – All driving directions begin something like this: "Start down Peachtree Street... and when you see the Waffle House..."*

Yes, I know there are stereotypes. I know you don't order beef tartare or blue fin tuna at

Waffle House. I know they aren't really restaurants – they are roadside diners – maybe the last of the species. I know they have struggled with racial issues in the past. I know they aren't perfect. But there are over a thousand of these things in 25 states – mostly in the South and the Midwest – annually serving enough sausage patties, that stacked together, would be four times taller than the Empire State Building. Every minute the restaurant chain serves 340 strips of bacon, 100 orders of grits, and 33 hamburgers. In the last 60 years, Waffle House diners have served nearly 1 billion waffles, 1.5 billion cups of coffee, 2 billion orders of hash browns, and 3 billion orders of eggs and omelets. What they do, they do right, and we can learn something from them, and learn it in a way that sticks in our hearts like their grease droppings stick in our veins.

To get the griddle warmed up, here are a few things that I have learned about "The Gospel According to Waffle House:"

> *No matter who you are and no matter what time of day it is, the door is always open. They may not have everything you like on the menu, but you will find something on the menu that you like.*

*The coffee is always fresh and the music is always good.*
*Visit all the great restaurants in the world, and still, you will never sit with a more interesting or diverse crowd.*
*The place is often cramped, and it's hard to find a seat; but be patient, your spot will open up.*
*Few places offer such a great opportunity for locals and newcomers to meet one another. And good things happen when neighbors get together.*

It all began in 1949 when Joe Rogers bought a house from Tom Forkner in the Avondale Estates neighborhood of Atlanta, Georgia. The men became neighbors and good friends. Both had been in the restaurant business and had pursued other interests as well, but they wanted to own something for themselves – and share it with others. Joe and Tom wanted to create a restaurant focused on people; both their associates and their customers, and in the process serve good, fast food. They went to work on this idea and on Labor Day 1955 a Southern icon and American phenomenon was born.

Here is how Joe Rogers describes their business model: "We are not in the food business. We are in the people business." Remember that next time you walk into a Waffle House and that waitress that reminds of you of your crazy Aunt Shirley calls you "Hon," "Darling," or "Sweet Cheeks" twenty times before you leave the table. She is doing her job.

This is our first reminder of who we are and what we are about. This is chapter one, verse one of "The Gospel According to Waffle House:" We are not in the religion business. We are not in the church business. We are not in the institutional or organizational business. We are in the people business. It's about creating a welcoming environment for all who come. And if we expend all of our energy defending our opinions, drafting our policies, arguing about how we are right and everyone else is wrong, we risk ignoring those whom God has surrounded us with; those who need to know that there are no locks on the door, the lights are always left on, and the coffee is always pouring. "Come on in, you are welcome!"

This is Romans 15:2, 7-8. We will return to Paul's words in Romans 15 each week for this series (I'm not sure Paul would approve, but as much as he traveled, I'm sure he would have loved Waffle House):

17

*"Each one of us needs to look after the good of the people around us, asking ourselves, 'How can I help?' So reach out and welcome one another into God's glory. Jesus did it; now you do it! Jesus, staying true to God's purposes, reached out in a special way to the Jewish insiders so that the old ancestral promises would come true for them. As a result, the non-Jewish outsiders have been able to experience mercy and to show appreciation to God, [so that] outsiders and insiders, may rejoice together" (The Message)!*

Paul wrote the book of Romans to a group of Christians with whom he had no personal association. He was going to visit them at some point in the future, and this letter is an introduction, an appeal for help and prayer, a theological discourse, and contains some practical instruction for following the way of Jesus. The congregation in Rome could not have been very large at the time – though it would eventually become the center of Christianity for the next 1500 years – and it was made up of mostly Jewish converts to Christianity. This was not unusual; Jesus was a good Jew and so were Paul and all of the early disciples. But as Paul writes here, it is after an incredible sea change in the church. Non-Jews, or Gentiles – in the version of the Bible I just read they are called outsiders – had begun converting to Christ in incredible numbers.

This produced a good deal of angst in the earliest formation of the church. Since they were all Jews, there were all of these social, racial, and religious boundaries in place, boundaries that had been there for centuries. Now Jesus comes along, with all his disciples who couldn't stop squawking and scribbling about him, and they are all saying the same thing: "Those barriers have been removed. There's no more Jew or Gentile, no more man or woman, no more rich or poor." Jesus accepts all who come to him, and has uniquely integrated humanity – we are all in the same family.

If you are "in Christ" to use Paul's favorite phrase, you have a blood connection, Jesus' shed blood, with all others who are in Christ. The door has been opened to all, and for those already a part of the family, it is their job – and our job – to say, "How can I help? Let me welcome you in. I've been around long enough to be an insider. I sort of know the ropes and the routine. Come on in and let me show you around."

This is one of the more amazing blind spots that we in Western Christianity have. We have so made the gospel about getting saved; getting in; avoiding eternal damnation; having a "personal relationship with Jesus Christ," that we have missed the communal and corporate aspect of the gospel. In Christ, God has created a new family, a new way of living in the world. People – all people – really count to God. They are really welcomed by God. They are really wanted in God's family. The Christian vocation, then, extends well beyond what we might call evangelism – getting people to pray a mechanical prayer – to inviting people to see that they now fit into God's new universe, something Jesus called the Kingdom of God, of which the church is a part.

So, we don't reject others, we receive them. We don't alienate, we invite. We don't divide, we embrace. We don't slam the door in peoples' faces, we hold the door open. Why? Because this is how God treats people. We say, "We are a part of God's family – but so are you – come on in, the table is spread." Genuinely welcoming people into our home, surrounding them with love and calling them family is what we are to be about.

To believe in a holy God is to believe in a God with open arms to all who will come. It is to give up on protecting our turf and our purity. It is to set aside our fears and what we perceive as threatening. It is to open ourselves up to be open to others. Who we are and what we are about begins with this phrase, already read: "We will be a community of faith." God is about creating open, welcoming communities that invite people in. We aren't in the church business. We are in the people business.

The question is obvious. I'm asked it from time to time: "So, are you running one of those churches that make it easy for people to get in?"

First, I'm not running anything. Most of the time I'm barely hanging on, like a green cowboy that has caught the worst bull in the lot. It's an adventure! And second, I'm not in the church business, though I sometimes use the word, "church." And third, yes, that's exactly the kind of place I hope this is: A place where it is easy to get in. There, I said it. Quote me. I want this to be a place with no locks on the doors, no bars on the windows, and no one guarding the communion table to determine who is worthy or unworthy. I want this to be a place where all are welcome to worship God, learn what it means to follow Jesus, and be motivated and empowered to serve their neighbors.

I want people to leave here every week prepared to make accusations against us. I imagine they would go something like this:

*"That group isn't clear enough in everything they believe, but they really believe in Jesus...*

*"Well, I thought they were just a bit irreverent, but they sure did seem to care about one another...*

*"That place is just too non-traditional, but people do seem to matter to them...*

*"I just don't know about that preacher in the blue jeans, that fuzzy, redheaded guy, and that crazy band, but I know that's a group of people that love me."*

I want people to leave here each week full and stuffed to the gills, like they have just been to Waffle House. Just imagine it: People stumble out of our "scattered, smothered, and covered" time together. They've just about been killed with Southern-fried kindness. Twenty people kissed them on the cheek and asked, "How's your mama doin'?" and meant it. Three people called them "Hon." The music playing out of the jukebox was a little too loud for digestion, but it was good nonetheless. The bathroom is too small and there is only one, but how much time do you really spend in a bathroom anyway? The coffee was strong. The conversation was invigorating. The crowd was gloriously unusual. All the regulars were there and a bunch of folks I didn't know. And people are so full, they have to leave to go "work it off" in the coming week.

I've been doing some kind of ministry or church or whatever this is called for over 20 years (don't let my youthful looks fool you, now), and for the majority of that time I participated in a system and with an attitude that made it hard on people to get to God. In the words of Jesus to the Pharisees, "I loaded people down with unbearable religious demands and never lifted a finger to ease the burden. I shut the door of the Kingdom of Heaven in people's faces." Why? Because they weren't good enough, perfect enough, committed enough, straight enough, white enough, wealthy enough, or healthy enough. Or then, in those moments of clarity and conviction when I knew what I should do, I often didn't because I didn't want to fight about it in the deacon's meeting, offend the person with the thickest checkbook, or get fired.

God forgive me. God forgive us all for acting or behaving that way, and God give us the courage, that when we say "It's personal; it's about people; all are welcome," that we mean it and we aim to live it.

I'll conclude with a note from John Acuff. John, according to his biography, had eight jobs in eight years. He wanted to be an author, but wound up writing advertising for The Home Depot and companies like Bose and Staples. His hopes became a reality when he landed his dream job: Full-time writer on the Dave Ramsey team in 2010.

He writes for Dave, magazines, blogs, and has published three books. Good for him; he's just a nice guy. His first book, and the name of his blog are entitled, *Stuff Christians Like*. It is all satire and humor, poking fun at the church and Christians, because he himself is one. It is usually pretty funny. But occasionally he blogs something serious; something that is so spot-on, it can't be ignored. This is one of those things.

John's Catholic friend attended "Our Lady of Lourdes Catholic Church" in Daytona Beach, Florida while on vacation. The church hands out a bookmark to all newcomers and John got a hold of one and posted a picture of it on his website. The post caught fire, got picked up all over the country, and everyone had an opinion about it (I wish we could turn everyone's ability to comment off, sometimes). Some hated it. Some loved it. Some thought it was condescending. For my part, I love it. Here it is:

> *"We extend a special welcome to those who are single, married, divorced, gay, filthy rich, dirt poor, and 'yo no habla Ingles.' We extend a special welcome to those who are crying new-borns, skinny as a rail or could afford to lose a few pounds. We welcome you if you can sing like Andrea Bocelli or like our pastor who can't carry a note in a bucket. You're welcome here if you're 'just browsing,' just woke up or just got out of jail. We don't care if you're more Catholic than the Pope, or haven't been in church since little Joey's Baptism.*
>
> *"We extend a special welcome to those who are over 60 but not grown up yet, and to teenagers who are growing up too fast. We welcome soccer moms, NASCAR dads, starving artists, tree-huggers, latte-sippers, vegetarians, and junk-food eaters. We welcome those who are in recovery or still*

*addicted. We welcome you if you're having problems or if you're down in the dumps or if you don't like 'organized religion,' we've been there too. If you blew all your offering money at the dog track, you're welcome here. We offer a special welcome to those who think the earth is flat, work too hard, don't work, can't spell, or because grandma is in town and she wanted to go to church.*

*"We welcome those who are inked, pierced or both. We offer a special welcome to those who could use a prayer right now, had religion shoved down your throat as a kid or got lost in traffic and wound up here by mistake. We welcome tourists, seekers and doubters, bleeding hearts … and you!"*

## Ω Ω Ω

Lord, make the doors of our hearts, our homes, and this community wide enough to receive all who need love and friendship. Make those same doors narrow enough to shut out all prejudice and pride. Help us to welcome the stranger, the other, the needy, the forgotten, and the poor; and in so doing, welcome your Son. Remind us that faith is personal. People matter. We make this prayer in the name of Jesus Christ, our Lord. Amen.

# TWO

## It's About People, Part 2

No discussion of any Southern icon, such as the Waffle House, would be complete without a reference to the late, great Lewis Grizzard. For the uninitiated who do not know who he was, shame on you. You should repent of your evil ways in sackcloth and ashes, beginning even now. In the summer of 1992, Lewis wrote a column about his experience at a local Waffle House entitled, "Gnawing Problem is Solved." I'll read a portion of that column here:

> *As I look back on my life, the Waffle House seems to have been one of the most consistent things in it. The Waffle House is always there at the next exit, always open,*

*always ready to throw on a couple of eggs for me and even an occasional T-bone steak. The Waffle House T-bone comes with a salad, hash browns, and two hamburger buns sliced and toasted. I know, it's white bread.*

*"If you eat too much white bread, Lewis, it will kill you."*

*I don't care. I was reared on white bread and I'm going to stay with it. Just get somebody to sing "Precious Memories" at my funeral. I pulled into Waffle House the other day and my waitress was named Kay, and she was pleasant — that's a consistent thing about Waffle House. They have good help.*

*I ordered a T-bone medium well. Kay wrote down my order and yelled it to the cook. He never responded, but Waffle House cooks never do. They can be frying six eggs, four pieces of bacon, and have two waffles in the iron at the same time and listen to three waitresses yelling out orders and it all registers; and they rarely get an order wrong.*

*My steak was cooked perfectly. I ate all the steak I could. But did you ever notice how much meat is left on a T-bone that you can't get to with a knife and fork? If you are eating at a fancy steak restaurant, you wouldn't dare think of picking up what's left of your steak and gnawing that good meat off the bone. But this is Waffle House. I called Kay over. "What is the Waffle House policy on a customer picking up what's left of his T-bone and gnawing the meat close to the bone?"*

*"Do whatever floats your boat," smiled Kay. I picked up my T-bone and happily gnawed away. The guy with the Harley Davidson T-shirt seated at the counter beside me never looked up; nobody in the entire Waffle House seemed offended. What a nice experience. It was just like home. Which is the only place I've ever picked up a steak and gnawed away at the bone. A precious memory at the Waffle House. Oh, how it lingers. Pass the white bread and put another quarter in the jukebox.*[1]

We are returning to this series entitled, "The Gospel According to Waffle House." Again, rather than dealing with mission statements, vision statements, and core values, in a moment of inspiration or stupidity, I turned instead to the Waffle House. We are gleaning what we can use from them, and applying it to us. Last week this was our premise: "It's about people." Remember, we are not in the religion business. We are not in the church business. We are not in the institutional business. We are in the people business. It's about creating a welcoming environment for all who come.

I didn't finish my thought last week about "the people business," so if I can follow the example of the illustrious Lewis Grizzard, and with your permission, I'd like to pick it up again and "gnaw away" at the meat still on the bone – that would "float my boat." Doing so, I'll return again to Waffle House co-founder Joe Rogers, who said, "Our mission is to deliver a unique experience where regular customers are greeted by name and enjoy social interaction with their servers and others."[2]

A unique experience? But what could be more mundane than a Waffle House, really? Could anything be more ordinary than chopped potatoes and scrambled eggs; or a T-bone steak you can buy for $7? Is there a place in the whole American culinary cosmos that is less of an adventure? Old, wooden, press-board booths that can't be adjusted and strike your back at all the wrong places? Menus that double as your placemats? A yellow logo that is stale and dated? Yet, we know all of this going in the door, don't we? And in all of this ordinariness, there is something unique, and true to the founder's intentions. It becomes a place that you do not simply visit; it becomes something that you experience, and exceptionally so. It becomes something that you share with others.

That is the nature of an experience. You participate in it by receiving and then sharing it with others: Receiving and sharing. A restaurant that receives people in but does not share the experience of good food with them, is not going to be in business for long. Restaurants whose patrons receive food but aren't invigorated enough to encourage others to come to the table and experience it for themselves, aren't going to last. I can say it like this: Waffle House doesn't exist for itself. It exists for others. It creates unique experiences, not for the sake of uniqueness, but to feed others.

The church is no different. We receive people in, and we send them out. We take in resources and we get rid of them. We invite people to dine at the table, and then we kick them out the door to share what they have experienced. Creating a church isn't the end. It is a means to bless and serve the world. A church that takes in people but does not share the experience of good food with them, is not going to be "in business" for long. Churches whose attendees receive food but aren't invigorated enough to encourage others to come to the table, aren't going to last. There is giving and taking, receiving and sharing.

Here is what sometimes happens, I think: Churches become narcissistic and self-centered. They focus all of their energy and resources upon themselves, leaving little if anything at all, for the greater community. But the church was never intended to be a self-absorbed, therapeutic organization where its members are obsessed with navel gazing or obsessing about their own spiritual needs. Churches were never meant to devolve into collections of self-interested people looking for their next spiritual spoon-fed meal or having their "needs met." The church is not a "What's in it for me?" society. The church is here for others, for the community, and for the world.

Churches can become a good deal like the musical, "Little Shop of Horrors." Have you ever seen the musical or the movie adaptation?[3] It's a dark little picture about a florist named Seymour who has this little, hungry, Venus Fly Trap flower whose appetite is for blood, and it cannot be sated. The flower, from outer space if I recall correctly, gets hungrier and hungrier crying out all the time, "Feed me, Seymour!" And it wants to feed on people! Now, it didn't begin that way. The little plant's uniqueness actually saved the flower shop. It became the centerpiece of the entire operation making everyone so happy, even wealthy. But over time it came to consume everything and everybody.

How many churches go through this same type of deterioration? How many have lost their way because they have turned inward? They have developed self-absorbed appetites that devour all the resources that the church can muster. They eat up their best assets and their best people. Of course, it didn't start that way. What they started with was successful. It made everybody happy, even wealthy. But the growing self-centeredness finally leaves nothing for those who need it the most – those outside the walls of the sanctuary. Oh, maybe there are a few fruit baskets for the poor at Christmas time, but everything is consumed within, and nothing is left.

This type of thinking and behavior is corrected by some of the old sanctuaries of my childhood. There was a sign over the back door that we read every week when we exited. It said, "Enter to worship. Leave to serve." The church's worship must launch us into the world with the love of God. This is the only way the church can live – it is the only thing that keeps us alive. To do one without the other is to approach our vocation half-heartedly.

Going further, consider the word we sometimes use to describe worship: "Liturgy." Liturgy means, literally, "public worship." It is "worshipful service." In the more "liturgical" traditions, those churches focus on a book of worship to guide them. They observe the church calendar, the *Book of Common Prayer* maybe, they decorate their sanctuaries with the proper colors for the proper seasons of the year. It's very ordered. It's very manageable, and it's all very good. This is what some of us think of when we hear the word, liturgy. That, or we think of reciting the Apostles' Creed which is very good as well. But let me challenge that thinking, somewhat.

Liturgy comes from two Greek words, *laos* and *ergon*; meaning "people" and "work." Liturgy is the "work *of* the people" and it is the "work *for* the people." In Roman society, to build a bridge for public use, especially if on one's private property, was called a liturgy. If someone took on military or public service at his own expense, it was considered liturgical. Wealthy patrons of the arts would often sponsor huge plays, theatrical dramas, and musicals – simply to share this artistic beauty with the public – and they called these gatherings, liturgies.

Following this reasoning, Rodney Clapp argues that the liturgy of the church should always be related to service, as the church builds bridges at its own expense, and invites the world to cross over; as the church serves the public and foots the bill; as the church invites all who will come to witness and participate in the beauty of God's salvation; as the church provides all the means and resources for the artistry of grace to be experienced.[4] A liturgy isn't just a verse read from a book or a gathering under a steeple. It is service of God's people, and by God's people, *for* the people of our community.

And going further still. Last week my beleaguered Atlanta Falcons won a playoff game. I shouted and rejoiced like I'd just got saved at a tent meeting, for I have long borne the weight of that franchise's sin and shortcomings. And here we are this week, facing the biggest game of the year – of the last decade. In just a few hours the team will circle up in what we call a "huddle." Now, this is not time wasted, is it? No. When the team huddles, it is preparing itself to execute a play. The huddle is the preparation to that end.

Really, the only reason a team takes the time to huddle is to ready itself to play the game. So the huddle is necessary, but if all a team does is huddle, it won't be much of a game. What will make or break the game is when the huddle is broken. Then, can the team do something on the field?

On Sunday mornings many of us charge out of the locker room suited up in our best clean and pressed uniforms. We sing our fight songs and wave our banners. We even tailgate together down at the buffet line. We gather in our holy huddles to plan and plot, but most of us never actually play. That we have fulfilled our religious duty of going to church, that we attended the weekly pep rally seems to be enough for the team. But what happens inside our sanctuaries and houses of worship week after week, while important, is not where the game is actually played.

Our weekly gatherings are more like locker room speeches.

They are weight rooms that strengthen our spiritual muscles.

They are rehab facilities in which we can get healthy.

They are nutritional centers to feed our bodies.

But when our muscles are strong, our

wounds bandaged, and our hearts motivated, we have to leave the huddle and get out there on the field where the game is actually played. So it really doesn't matter how long, how often, or how inspiring our holy huddles are. What matters is this: When we break the huddle have we been empowered to actually deliver the goods on the field?

Listen, what we do here on Sundays, is fairly easy. It's easy for you, and I'm glad. I want you to be here. I want you to feel welcome. I want you to want to come to this gathering. I work very hard to do my part; to be ready; to be prepared; to, in the words of my mentor, "Have something to say, not just have to say something."[5] But this is where worship, service, and mission begin. It is not where these things end. Anybody can get a decent preacher, some toe-tapping music, a chorus line, and draw a crowd. I'm much more concerned with what this crowd does once we disperse.

I'm so glad to be back here, but this isn't about me. It's not about you. It's about people who aren't here!

So, I'm just a florist, a gardener, trying to be aware of those plants and practices that might consume us, and trimming them back when I have to, so that our focus stays where it should.

I'm just a structural engineer, trying to build the bridges of service and mercy to a world that needs those things, and racking the construction budget and plan to make sure it's not a bridge to nowhere.

I'm just a football coach who gives locker room speeches. I don't even get to play in the game like some of you do, but I'll do my best and try to coach you to do the same.

I'm just the fry cook in the kitchen. I'll try to rustle up some of the most filling food you can eat. It won't be fancy, but it will be good, I hope. And when you have cleaned your plate, "You ain't gotta go home, but you can't stay here." Take what you have received and share it with others.

So while I want people to come to church, I don't want to import as many into the sanctuary as possible. I want to export as many people as possible into the community.

We should meet the needs of our congregation, but we can't fall for the capitalistic trick of creating goods and services for church shoppers; we must concentrate on doing good service in the world.

We cannot maintain a "come and see" attitude, though I hope many will come and see; it is much preferred – it is much more biblical – if we "go and be" the church.

> *"I went to church on Sunday."* Good for you, but big deal. Did you become the church on Monday morning where you work, live, and play?
>
> *"I was treated to a good sermon today."* I hope so! But how did you treat the people around you as a result of that sermon?
>
> *"I tell you, that music just filled my heart so that I could hardly stand it!"* Okay, but did you empty that full heart out for those who have not had the same experience?

It's about people – the ones that are here, right now today; but more so, it's about the people who aren't here, and those who may never darken the door of this place. We receive, but it is for the sake of sharing with others.

Now, if someone says something like I did last week, something that pertains to openness, grace, and mercy toward others, one should expect that such talk will be tested. I must confess that within 24 hours of my ooey-gooey, good-vibes, lovin'-feelin' talk last Sunday, I had thrown it all away. Cindy called me on Monday from Georgia experiencing some difficulty at the doctor's office. She couldn't get our son's medication. Our son Bryce has taken a certain ADHD medication for seven years and he cannot live without it. More to the point, we and his teachers cannot live without him having it. It's no shame. A writing friend of mine wrote on her blog recently that "All you need is Jesus is a lie; sometimes you need a little Zoloft too."[6] Amen.

Anyway, I said to Cindy, "I'll handle it." I called and it began well, but then I was put on hold for 15 minutes. I called again, and with a little more passion, communicated my frustrations. I was then told that they had talked to my wife and it had been handled. "No it has not," I said, and I could feel that ugly little ogre I keep locked in the basement of my heart stomping up the stairs to unlock the door to my mouth. Somehow I got transferred to a third nurse named Amanda. I let Amanda have it with all the sarcasm and scorn I could muster.

She said, "Sir, there's no need to be rude."

To which I responded: "I am not being rude. I'm 400 miles away, trying to help both my wife and my son, and I'm simply stating the facts as I understand them: Your office maintains a profound level of constant incompetency!"

She hung up on me.

The ogre had control over my entire being at that point. In the parking lot of the Donut Hole Restaurant I turned into a gamma-ray infected, green-skinned, raging animal that would have made The Hulk blush. Eventually I got the script written, though it wasn't pretty. About an hour later I called back and asked for Amanda. I said, "Amanda, this is Ronnie McBrayer." She audibly groaned. I said, "I need to apologize for my attitude and my words. It was not fair for you to bear the brunt of my frustration. You may not accept my apology, but I have to give it nonetheless or I won't sleep for a week. I was wrong. I'm sorry." Amanda then offered me what I needed: Grace. She forgave me. Our entire animus evaporated and we had a wonderful, much healthier conversation.

Here is the test of a business model committed to people:

We don't just say that people are welcome. We act that way.

We don't just care for the people who are here, but we use what happens here, to care for those out there.

And when we fail to live up to our calling and share grace with others – and we will! – we admit it, confess it, and make it right.

People matter. If we are going to believe and live the gospel – even the "Gospel According to Waffle House" – it begins right there.

## Ω Ω Ω

Almighty God, give to us, and then send out from us, many who will be shaped after your heart and who will hold firmly to your great love. To us and through us, give grace to those who most need it; give strength to the weak; give faithfulness to the strong; give aid to the poor; and give guidance to the seeker, that together we might all follow you. In Christ we pray, Amen.

# THREE

## It's About Identity

Contrary to what some of you might think, I am not a paid spokesperson for the Waffle House chain of restaurants. I'm not even getting a free cup of coffee because of this series of talks. Sincerely, I hope this series, "The Gospel According to Waffle House," has stirred your imagination a bit. I hope it has caused you to think about this thing we call church. I hope it bears some long-term consequences among us. And I hope it will make a connection between something we know very well – eating at a roadside diner – and something we may not know very well at all – what theologians call ecclesiology: That is, the nature of the church.

What is the church?

What is the church's character?

Why does the church do what it does?

And I hope that when you see the familiar black and yellow logo of Waffle House, for the rest of your life, you will think about your vocation as a follower of Jesus.

So, we turn to a third "meal" in this series. The first two were on the subject of people. "The Gospel According to Waffle House" is a gospel about people. People matter to God. He loves them. He welcomes them in – all people – and so should we. Today we turn to another item on the menu, but before we do, I'd like to share that I'm not the only one inspired by Waffle House these days.

Here are a couple of paintings that an artist rendered last year of the Waffle House (These paintings were shown via projection during the talk; one is included as a cover images for this e-book, with permission from and gratitude to the artist). I love these, and the main reason is because the artist is our very own Sean Dietrich (Sean leads the A Simple Faith's Sunday worship band, affectionately known as "Sawmill Gravy and the Biscuits"). In addition to his masterful skills at the piano and behind the microphone, Sean is quickly becoming an accomplished painter (Visit Sean's website at www.seandietrich.com).

I'm not a prophet, and I'm definitely not an art critic, but I predict that Sean will excel at painting in a way that will exceed even his musical abilities. I say this because just as with Sean's music, this artistic talent comes natural to him. I don't mean to embarrass him, but all this music and art is inside of him. It lurks about in his brain beneath all that contrary red hair, and all it needs is expression. All it needs is a doorway to the outside world, and out it comes: Out of his mouth, through his hands to the keyboard, a flash at the end of his paintbrush, and alive on his sketchpad.

He requires – and this is not fair – very little work to be good at what he does. Yet, this is exactly why he works so hard at it. Because he isn't trying to produce something, manufacture something, or work up a piece of music or art that isn't there. It's already there! His task is to hone the skills of *transmission*. His work is to take all that substance within, and let it pass as purely as possible, to others.

Letting the supernatural goodness within flow to others;

Refusing to artificially manufacture something that isn't already inside of us;

Honing our skills of transmission, so that who we are can simply get out: This is the third serving of "The Gospel According to Waffle House."

The founders of the Waffle House chain said it like this: "Our ambition is not to get bigger. It is to get better."[7] They were saying, and they have lived by this, "Our plan isn't for big growth. We don't target markets and demographics and seek to expand beyond our abilities. We just *are*. We are going to concentrate on doing what we do, being who we are, and delivering the highest quality possible in our restaurants, and if expansion is the natural result, then so be it, but that is not the aim."

"The Gospel According to Waffle House" is about being better, not bigger. It's quality, not quantity. It's goodness over growth. It's realness instead of results. It is about substance, not success. And, for our purposes today: It's not about increasing, it is about identity.

Again, we take our cues from Romans 15. Remember that Paul is coming to the end of a magnificent letter written to the Christians in the city of Rome. It was likely a small church, just getting started, and very far removed from the centerpiece of Western Christianity that it would become. Much of the letter has been doctrinal — what Paul believed and what he preached – and it is much beloved. Romans 8, particularly these questions at the end of the chapter: "If God is for us who can be against us? Who can make accusation against those whom God has chosen as his own? What can separate us from the love of God?"

These questions, and the answers Paul provides, are some of the best words ever written on paper. Paul provides lots of answers for this fledgling church, and here in chapter 15, as he wraps up, he turns his answers to more practical matters.

In these verses he reports on how his work is going. He's been traveling across three continents, planting churches, starting Jesus groups, teaching the Bible – and the Gentiles, those who were outsiders and considered unworthy of God's love – have been coming to Christ in great numbers. It is a sea change in the composition and nature of the early church. He's telling the Romans, "People all over the world are getting in on this – they are getting what you already have!" And what do they have? Paul tells them that they are full of "goodness." This is Romans 15:14-15:

*"I am fully convinced, my dear brothers and sisters, that you are full of goodness.*

*You know these things so well you can teach each other all about them. Even so, I have been bold enough to write about some of these points, knowing that all you need is this reminder" (NLT).*

That's a unique word in the original language, the word "goodness." It's only used four times in the entire New Testament, and each time it is used exclusively by the Apostle Paul. He regards it as a "fruit of the spirit." His most exhaustive listing of the fruit of the spirit is found in Galatians 5. There he says, "The Holy Spirit produces this kind of fruit in our lives: love, joy, peace, patience, kindness, goodness, faithfulness, gentleness, and self-control. There is no law against these things" (Galatians 5:22-23, NLT)!

Paul is writing in shorthand, telling the Romans the same thing he told the Galatians, that they have been given God's very Spirit, and it produces all of this wonderful fruit. All they have to do is let it out! Share it with one another, he says. "You know to do that. You know how to do that. I just want to remind you to hone the skills that will permit God's goodness within you to get out."

It's as if he is saying, "You are musicians with the music already in your heads. Play it.

Allow it to make your fingers move across the instruments. You are vocalists tuned to perfect pitch. Just sing. You are artists who have this gift within you – God gave it to you – pick up the brush and paint. Let it flow out. The work is not producing something that isn't there, the only work is letting it pass from you to others. God has blessed you with it! Use it!"

Maybe I should say it this bluntly: "Quit trying to be something you are not, and just be who you are."

Now, I could take those last few words and preach the rest of my life on them. If we each concentrated our energies and lives on being who God has made us to be, using what God has blessed us with, rather than creating these façades of who we wished we were, or who we thought we ought to be, or who others want us to be, the world would be a happier place, and we would be happier people. But for today, let me apply these words to our collective selves – to our church – and do what Paul did, remind us of what we already know. This is for us:

*If we attempt to be something we are not, we will be nothing.*

*If we cave in to the temptation of image management, becoming what every other steeple-clad building is, at the expense of our unique voice and witness, it will be a price too high.*

*If we become infatuated by the smokescreen of bigger crowds, expanded market share, and a stronger bottom line, then we will not only lose our way; we will lose everything.*

*If we can't be happy just letting what is within us, what God has blessed us with, flow out to others, then we will never be happy.*

There is a nefarious danger that every congregation must face, the greatest internal threat imaginable: The desire for success. Go ask most churches – most of us – this question: "What do you want your church to do?" And the answer will probably be, "More." We want the church to get bigger. We want the church to be more prosperous. We want the church to be superior to the one down the street. More, more, more.

The head-counters want more people in the pews.

The bean-counters want more money in

the offering plates.

The preachers want a bigger empire over which to preside.

The denomination wants more victorious stories for their magazines.

The children's workers want more volunteers.

The planners want more programs.

The grounds committee wants more buildings.

These are the wrong answers! Why? Because "What do you want your church to do?" is the wrong question! The right question is this: "Who are we?" It has to begin right there; questions of identity, calling, vocation, and purpose – not questions of activity, goal-setting, and achievement. Start with the wrong questions, and the answers will take us to the wrong places.

I wrote a column a few years ago that gets right after this. The column recently made its way into Luther Seminary's, *Renew 52: 50+ Ideas to Revitalize Your Congregation from Leaders under 50.*[8] It is an eccentric collection of essays, and it's now a free e-book download, available at Luther Seminary. My essay is entitled "McDonaldization." Here's a part of it:

*"McDonaldization" is a word first*

*coined by sociologist George Ritzer to describe American culture. The predictable, robotic means of producing hamburgers and fries, according to Ritzer, has overtaken our society. Like one giant automated system everything from fast food to childcare to education rolls off the assembly line to be delivered to the consumer for the saving of time, money, and effort… Scottish theologian John Drane has rightly applied the term to contemporary spirituality… We have so motorized, organized, and institutionalized the church that songs, sermons, programs, and prayers just roll off the spiritual assembly line…*

*Raise the sanctified golden arches and use whatever method will deliver the goods… Just get the right preaching, the right music, adequate parking, proper advertising, and the most alluring programs. Then people will surely flock to the campus. But is this even the point? What if efficiently "succeeding" isn't the goal at all? What if having the biggest and finest crowd isn't the primary objective? What if our carefully controlled, mass produced spirituality ends up being a distraction to true growth?*

*Instead, what if the goal is for us to learn to be partners together on this journey of following and becoming like Christ? What if the goal is to be the unique, counter-cultural, community of God? What if the goal is to love our neighbor and aid people in becoming who they were created to be?*

I'll add right here that McDonald's is worse now than when I first wrote that essay. I was in one the other day (and as an aside, I must admit that since they put the calorie count next to their menu items, I've ordered a few less combo meals!), and it's like *The Matrix* in there! Cups drop out of a rack, are filled by a machine with a pre-measured quantity of ice. Then they follow a mini-conveyor belt to the cola dispenser delivering a premeasured shot of carbonation. All the worker must do is put a lid on it. The salt shaker is preloaded so that the fry cook can't over shake the spuds. The condiments for your burger are shot out of what looks like a caulk gun. There are no adjustments or knobs on any of the appliances. You just push buttons and the machines take care of everything for we drones standing in line. Everything is premeasured, preplanned, and predetermined.

Contrast that with your local Waffle House, your local diner, or a homegrown burger joint. You place your order with a lady named Shelby or Wynona. She writes it down on a pad of paper and yells it to the cook. The cook hand prepares your meal just for you! There are no digital displays. There are no buttons to push. Your coffee or your Coke is running down the side of the cup with all its stickiness, because they filled the cup with their own hands. Sometimes your burger has too much ketchup or not enough mustard – that's okay – somebody actually gave their time and attention to it. You're served on a real plate, not a Styrofoam clamshell laced with BPAs. And when it's time to go, you pay in cash. No swiping, pin-coding or Near Field Communicating. It's slower. It's not as convenient. It might even cost a little more, but I think it is worth it.

Granted, McDonald's is a lot more successful than your local diner! It's bigger – much bigger! It has restaurants in 119 countries. It serves 62 million people a day. 88% of the world recognizes the symbol of the Golden Arches (only 60% recognize the Christian cross). McDonald's distributes more toys a year than Wal-Mart or Toys-R-Us. And you can't stand anywhere in the continental United States and be more than 100 miles from a McDonald's.

Waffle House? Forget it. They have only a few hundred locations, tiny by comparison. They can barely get out of the South. And your local diner? It's smaller still, and how can its $250,000 annual budget match Ronald McDonald who has the 90th largest economy in the world? A multi-site, multi-national, corporation that seeks to colonize the entire world – this is success! This is what we want our churches to be!

Well count me out.

Listen, I like a quarter pounder with cheese as much as the next sheep in line, but I much prefer being treated as a human being and not as a statistic who is nothing more than a figure in an actuary's spreadsheet. Understand:

I am not anti-growth. I am pro-mission.

I am not anti-expansion. I am pro-identity.

I am not anti-success. I am pro-substance.

I am not anti-planning and process. I am pro-purpose.

I hope A Simple Faith continues to grow. I hope we burst at the seams, and I look forward to working out all the good problems that such growth produces. But growing a bigger crowd is not the objective. Fulfilling our unique vocation as a community of faith that will simply, and in uncomplicated fashion, worship God, follow Christ, and serve the world, is the objective. Building the next "big thing," developing religious goods and services to attract church shoppers, or trying to get as many people as possible to take on as much religious responsibility as possible is not our ambition. Being a safe and substantial place of grace for those who have never given faith a shot, and for those who thought they had no more faith left, is the ambition.

Putting all of our energies and emphases on well-polished worship services, a strategic growth plan, or fund-raising campaigns is not something I have energy for! But holding forth a profound trust in God, looking to Christ as the best way to live in this world, learning to love and serve those around us, and welcoming all who are looking for friendship, liberation, and rest is exactly where, and exactly how, I want to spend my life and energy. If growth is the result of this mission – this identity we are living out – then thanks be to God for it. In the meantime we will be true to ourselves and our calling.

In conclusion, and cleaning off today's

table, I have to say that this little series about the Waffle House almost didn't come to fruition – it was almost a meal left unserved – because my first thought was, "That is ridiculous." And maybe it is. So while much of the content would have been the same, it was almost called "The Gospel According to Alcoholics Anonymous."

Frederick Buechner famously said, "What happens in A.A. is far closer to what Christ meant his Church to be, and what it first was, than the Church today."[9] Amen, to that, and I'm going to circle back to this at some point in the future, but here I must make reference to one of the traditions in the 12-Step Program. There are 12 steps, and there are 12 traditions in A.A. The 12 steps are for the individuals trying to get sober. The 12 traditions are for the group. The 12 traditions form the group's identity.

They really are brilliant. Here are a few of the traditions:

> *"The common welfare should come first; personal recovery depends upon unity."*
> *"For our group purpose there is but one ultimate authority; a loving God as He may express Himself."*
> *"Each group has but one primary*

*purpose: To carry its message to those who still suffer."*

*"Our group ought never endorse, finance or lend its name to any related facility or outside enterprise, lest problems of money, property and prestige divert us from our primary purpose."*

Do you see why I love these?! But here is the one most applicable today. It is Tradition Eleven in the Big Blue Book of A.A: *"Our public relations policy is based on attraction rather than promotion."*

No one goes out and spends a trillion dollars on promoting and marketing Alcoholics Anonymous (and you'll never see Waffle House do so either). You just hang out that familiar sign and get to work being who you are. Those who need it, will be attracted to it.

So let us recommit ourselves, beginning today, to being true to our vocation, not to building a bigger church. Let us foster the goodness within, not the growth without. Let us be about the substance of faith, not the success of our plans. Let us concentrate on attraction rather than promotion. And let us share the love of Christ by living out the unique identity God has given us, for if we cannot say it with the lives we live, then we cannot say it at all.

## Ω Ω Ω

Heavenly Father, plant the seeds of your good word within us. Make it alive, powerful, and effective in our hearts, producing much fruit. And may that fruit bear the power of attraction that you, through Jesus, would be honored. It's in Jesus' name we pray, Amen.

# FOUR

## It's About Simplicity

Imagine with me, if you would, a hot, muggy August day not too many years in the future. It is a small Gulf Coast town, not unlike our own. The thermometer reads nearly three digits with high humidity. Huge, billowing cumulus clouds hang in the blue sky. The wind is stiff and fiery; but there is hardly a leaf rustling in the trees, because there are very few leaves left on the trees. A Category 4 hurricane made landfall two days earlier. There is no power, no air conditioning, no gasoline, and very little ice. While there is extensive damage, thankfully, there are few injuries because everyone heeded the evacuation orders and skedaddled just in the nick of time (now we are really using our imaginations!).

Arriving on this scene of devastation is FEMA Regional Director for the Southeastern United States, Major Phillip May. He and his team have been prepping at the Federal Regional Response Center in Thomasville, Georgia, and now that the storm has passed, they are on site with their boots in the sand. They set up assistance stations. They search damaged homes. They coordinate with local and state authorities. They begin taking applications for federal assistance. They hold regular news conferences about the progress of the early recovery, and Major May and his staff go eat at the local Waffle House.

Here is a bit of useful Waffle House trivia for you: In times of disaster in the Southeast – hurricanes, tornadoes, and floods – FEMA now invokes what they call "The Waffle House Index."[10] This index was informally adopted after the severe hurricane seasons of the early 2000s. FEMA workers noticed that there was a correlation between the operations of the local Waffle House, and how bad conditions really were on the ground. FEMA administrator Craig Fugate said afterward, "If you get [to the scene of the disaster] and the Waffle House is closed, that's really bad. That's where you go to work." So this three-tiered Waffle House

Index was developed, as an unceremonious way of assessing storm damage:

*Green: The Waffle House has power, is staffed, and is serving a full menu. This means that damage is localized to a small area or overall damage is limited.*

*Yellow: The Waffle House has sketchy or generator-based power, and the menu is limited to only certain items. This means the damage is more extensive or covers a greater area and a more robust response will be required.*

*Red: The Waffle House is closed. The damage, somewhere in the affected region, is catastrophic.*

But why choose Waffle House for this Index? Well, they are always open – and when they are not – something is obviously wrong. But more to the point: The Waffle House has a very simple, uncomplicated, unsophisticated operation plan. There are very few moving parts. Food, less than a half-dozen workers fulfilling only a few major roles, power, gas, and water: If they have these, the restaurant is up and running. Even without some of these things; without power, without a full staff, without all the necessary items to round out a complete menu, the doors will open and the coffee will be pouring.

Here is the third course of this meal we have been digesting entitled, "The Gospel According to Waffle House." It is "Simplicity."

> This is Romans 15:20-21: *"My ambition has always been to preach the Good News where the name of Christ has never been heard, rather than where a church has already been started by someone else. I have been following the plan spoken of in the Scriptures, where it says, 'Those who have never been told about him will see, and those who have never heard of him will understand'"* (NLT).

I want us to think about simplicity along three lines (each of these could be a talk in and of themselves, but that wouldn't be in keeping things simple, would it?): Philosophically, organizationally, and theologically.

First, simplicity as a philosophy. One could say that Paul is a reductionist. For all his prolific writings and his wordiness at times, when pushed to answer the big questions, he reduces the complex to the simpler, more fundamental elements. Paul likes to flatten things out, making our vocation, calling, purpose, and life as the church together as modest as possible. Paul is an advocate of the "K.I.S.S." it principle. You know it: "Keep it short and simple." Or if you prefer, "Keep it simple, stupid." Of course there is a more elegant way of saying that: *Pluralitas non est ponenda sine necessitate.* That is, "Entities should not be multiplied unnecessarily."

That's a philosophical phrase from William Ockham who developed his ideas in the High Middle Ages, ideas we now call Ockham's Razor. Ockham's Razor, reduced to its simplest explanation is this (and it applies to mathematics, philosophy, government, management, and science): "All things being equal, the simplest solution is the best solution."

Albert Einstein, the most intellectual man this world has seen in centuries, has been credited with saying something like this: "Any intelligent fool can make things bigger and more complex... It takes a touch of genius to move toward simplicity; for the one who understands a subject the best is the one who can explain it the plainest."

Pauline reductionism, the "K.I.S.S." it principle, Ockham's Razor, Einstein Simplicity – these are things we all use, most every day, and very few of us are philosophers or mathematicians. Here is a common example, right from an undergraduate philosophy class: If someone asks me, "Excuse me, could you direct me to the bathroom?" That could be an urgent request, so I answer as simply as possible. I don't say, "Why yes, if you proceed south down the center of the room for approximately 12 paces, a room measuring roughly 40 by 60 feet, on a foundation poured 15 inches thick with standard concrete and reinforced steel rebar meeting all post-1992 Florida building codes; and then turn 86 degrees toward the west and matriculate through the double doors, doors purchased at the Home Depot in Panama City Beach circa November 2010 at a cost of $1,160 pre-tax.

"Once outside the stucco-finished building, turn once again to the south and advance to the conjunction of the north-south and east-west walls of said building at precisely 17 feet above sea level. At such time, being in full shade this time of year, and incidentally until the Spring Equinox, you will comfortably reverse your previous 86 degree turn, now pivoting toward the east. Maintaining this heading, you will arrive at an identical set of doors that you encountered previously, but this is not the same set. Enter the building at such time. Once in the foyer of the building (*foyer* is a French word, by the way, adapted to English during the building of the great European cathedrals), you will see appropriate gender-based signage directing you to the facilities that you require."

No! I'd say, "Go down the aisle, and take a left." Wouldn't I? Simplicity, from a practical and philosophical standpoint, cuts to the chase. It eliminates distractions and background noise. It jettisons all that is unnecessary and crucial. It makes things easier to access and easier to understand. So if I ask you what time it is, don't tell me how to build a clock. If I ask you where the water fountain is, don't explain to me the aqueduct system of the ancient Roman world. In the words of my crazy Uncle Donald who loves women and Bourbon – "Son, why you gotta reach around your elbow to scratch your ass?"

When in doubt or when facing competing solutions to a problem; when thinking about how to best live out our faith in the community; when organizing, mobilizing, and planning; the simplest answer is the best answer. The shortest distance between two points is still a straight line. This is more than a principle. It is a way of looking at ourselves, our work, our relationships, our faith, our vocation, and our world.

And this brings us to the second feature of simplicity: Organizational simplicity.

How I wish the church were different, but sometimes it can be utterly ridiculous in its structure. This is why I wish we had more time to talk about William Ockham. He was more than a philosopher. Centuries ahead of his time, he revolutionized the fields of logic, physics, and mathematics. He was one of the first Europeans to write about monarchial accountability, democratic government, and maybe the very first Catholic to bring up the subject of separation of church and state. He casts a long shadow. But missed in all this is an overlooked fact: Ockham was a theologian by trade. He was a monk. He was an English churchman. Why haven't we applied his philosophy of simplicity to the subject and entity he knew best – the church?

*Why do so many churches make it so hard to get in, and so easy to leave?*

*Why do so many churches build massive*

*theological explanations of their beliefs, but spend so little energy living those beliefs?*

*Why do some denominational structures still mirror the feudal system of Western Europe with Bishops, Archbishops and Cardinals taking the place of princes, earls and kings?*

*Why do some churches need enough organizational documents and charts to fill a shelf of 3-ring binders, if not three book shelves?*

*Why does a church of 200 people need 25 committees?*

*Why do some pastors demand that the people be more committed to the institution of a specific church, than the person of Jesus?*

*Why does the church organization drain people of their energy instead of setting them free to live and minister to others?*

*Why are church structures so brittle, so unassailable and unamendable?*

*Why can't we, the children of the*

*Reformation, do better at reforming our institutions?*

*Why does our traditionalism keep us from adapting to practical, everyday considerations?*

*Why are we more concerned with our container than the content of what's inside?*

*Why does church leadership allow good and godly people to kill themselves for the organization, instead of letting them live their lives for Christ?*

*Why do we allow organizational complication to distance us from the people we first organized to serve?*

This is an illustration I've spoken of in the past, and its use is obvious here. Some of the largest steam locomotives ever built were produced in the 1930s by the Lima Locomotive Company of Lima, Ohio. The granddaddy of them all was named the "Alleghany," and only two models of the dozen or so built survive. One of these survivors is stored at the Henry Ford Museum in Dearborn, Michigan. This beast weighs more than a million and a half pounds and has an output of 7,500 horsepower. In its short heyday it carried 25,000 pounds of coal and 100,000 pounds of water, but those resources could only power the engine for three hours. It had all this power and resources, but it took more than 90% of the engine's power just to move itself! Sure, it became much more efficient once it was moving, but the thing was so big, sucked up so much coal and water, and was so expensive to operate, it just wasn't practical.

The Lima Alleghany is an excellent, though painful, metaphor of most of our church and religious systems. We've got all the bells and whistles, steam is pouring out of the boiler, power is moving to the wheels, but most of it is spent just getting things moving. We spend most of our energy on ourselves, with little left to pull the load, as it were, along the tracks. And the resources we have been blessed with – in people, dollars, talent, influence and time – are all burned up and burned out at rates that are appalling. It has to be simpler than this. Maybe we can trade in our locomotive for a bicycle. We can't go as fast, and we can't carry as much baggage, but maybe that is exactly the point.

I say again, the church is not an end unto

itself, but is called as the people of God and imitators of Christ, to bless, serve, and love others. This servant task is unachievable if the church continues to spend its time, energy, resources, and personnel on building bigger, more complicated machinery, doctrines, and structures.

No, big isn't necessarily bad. Denominations aren't inherently evil. If you are a part of a mega-church you are not somehow missing out. None of these are corrupt, but complication, religious obstacles, and man-made roadblocks placed in the path of Christ – these are immoral. The commitment to spiritual simplicity always calls us to use severe discretion, and careful self-examination, to ensure that while the depth of our faith should always grow – faith is infinite in its depth – we should vigilantly purge ourselves of all the unnecessary structures that get attached to faith.

And a final aspect of simplicity: Theological simplicity.

Paraphrasing G.K. Chesterton, he said, "There are two ways to get enough. One is to get more. The other is to want less." With that, we revisit Paul's words to the Romans: "My ambition has always been to preach the Good News where the name of Christ has never been heard, rather than where a church has already been started by someone else. I have been following the plan spoken of in the Scriptures, where it says, 'Those who have never been told about him will see, and those who have never heard of him will understand.'"

What a simple, uncomplicated sense of vocation! And it's not the only time he said something like this. To the Corinthians he wrote, "When I first came to you, dear brothers and sisters, I didn't use lofty words and impressive wisdom to tell you God's secret plan. For I decided that while I was with you I would forget everything except Jesus Christ, the one who was crucified" (1 Corinthians 2:1-2, NLT).

And to the Philippians he said, "Everything else is worthless when compared with the infinite value of knowing Christ Jesus my Lord. For his sake I have discarded everything else, counting it all as garbage, so that I could gain Christ and become one with him" (Philippians 3:8, NLT). This concept of being "in Christ," or being "one" with him alone, is the crux of Pauline spirituality. He didn't want more, as in the Chesterton option. He wanted less. This kept him forgetting what was behind and pressing on toward knowing

Christ.

Isn't Christ enough for us, here? After all, what kind of people make up this congregation? Well, I image there are a few Calvinists in the room, if God has so predetermined that they be here. There are a number of Pentecostals not afraid to be seen with us, and we're not afraid of their spiritual rambunctiousness. There are practicing Catholics who sometimes attend Mass on Saturday night before coming here on Sunday morning. There are Episcopalians who go to early service there and then attend here later in the day. There's always representation from the good Lutherans, especially during snowbird season. There's more than a dozen Baptists, but I try to keep them separated from one another. When they get together I get nervous. There's an assembly from the Church of Christ but they have adapted to our musical instruments quite well. And there's a pile of Christian hippies and even one or two Unitarians.

We all come from rich, diverse, spiritual backgrounds. We've come together, not necessarily to escape our heritage, and not to add another item to our religious resumes; but to embrace less, because less is more.

So when I speak of theological simplicity,

I am not talking about dumbing down. I'm not trying to find the lowest common denominator and hoping that it will be enough to hold this loose confederation of pilgrims together. I'm not dismissing vigorous theological and spiritual exploration – far from it! I'm arriving, I hope, at the same conclusion as Paul: After working through the theological façades; having acquired all the diplomas, perfect attendance pins, and the certificates of merit, we ask this question: What good is all of this stuff if we lose focus on the One person who really matters? After you have worked through it all, and you get back to where faith began – with "Jesus loves me this I know, for the Bible tells me so" – you return more appreciative of that fact than ever before.

Consequently, you can go to other churches and maybe find more academic or theological rigor in the pulpit or the pew. But in a long tradition of seekers, from the Apostle Paul to the Franciscans, from the Anabaptists to the Quakers, from the religious orders of Catholicism to the European Reformers, we are spiritual simpletons. We have come to know this: There is a God to be worshipped (Lord knows that happens in a myriad of ways); there is Jesus to follow (we soak up his words and way – the red letters of the Gospel); and there is a world to be loved (and it's a world so big and so in need, we know we'll always have something to do).

And with that, I'll end where I began. A professor at Washington University has written an academic paper on the four companies in the United States that are most astute at disaster response. The professor lists Wal-Mart, Home Depot, Lowes, and Waffle House.[11] The first three are no surprise. They can do what they do out of sheer volume, and because they make a lot of money in the aftermath of a disaster. But the Waffle House, the academics say, is not a response business, and it has little to gain. They do it just because it is good business. They even have an Emergency Response vehicle named "EM-50" after Bill Murray's urban-assault vehicle from the movie "Stripes."

This vehicle shows up in affected areas to get their stores up and running as soon as possible. Why? Because people need a place to go after the storm. People need a meal in their stomach. They need to hear a familiar, comforting tune on the jukebox, and feel a blast of cold air-conditioning to tame the hot August air. They need to see their neighbors, drink a glass of Alice's Iced Tea (if the ice machine is back on), and quit eating out of a can with a plastic fork, waiting for the insurance adjuster to show up.

Storms will come as certain as the sunrise. Life will rend us to pieces. Disaster will strike. People's well-ordered, uninteresting routines will be suddenly dismantled. And when this happens, people go looking for a little help, a little sense and quiet in all the noisy fury. We can be that place. We can be that people, if we will do what we do, and be who we are, as simply and as straightforward as possible.

## Ω Ω Ω

"Dear God, occupy my heart with your tremendous Life. Let my eyes see nothing in the world but your glory, and let my hands touch nothing that is not for your service... Possess my whole heart and soul with the simplicity of love... that I may love not for the sake of merit, not for the sake of perfection, not for the sake of virtue, not for the sake of sanctity, but for you." Amen.[12]

RONNIE McBRAYER

# FIVE

## It's About Flexibility

A Hooters waitress, a Waffle House fry cook, and a Baptist preacher walk into a bar...

No, this is not the beginning of a very bad joke. The Hooters waitress was named Heather, the Waffle House cook was named Brad, and the Baptist preacher was yours truly. Heather and Brad made a striking couple – beautiful and handsome – and they had fallen in love. They asked me to do the honors of officiating their wedding, and I was happy to do so. Their nuptials were spoken well over a decade ago, and the couple, sadly, is no longer together. They are amiable friends now, and before their split produced a child as attractive as they are. Heather is no longer selling beer and hot wings – so a lot has changed – but Brad still works for Waffle House. In fact, he bought my family's dinner a few weeks ago. He's not a fry cook anymore. He is a district manager for one of North Georgia's largest Waffle House franchises.

Brad completed his education and was floundering about trying to land a career. It was then that a friend of his said, "Brad, you ought to come work with me at Waffle House. It's a great career and you'll make a killing." Well, the Waffle House was not on Brad's short list of dream vocations.

"The Waffle House?" he said. "I'm too smart for that. And besides, I have all my teeth."

But his friend persisted, and Brad eventually caved in. He donned the brown polyester pants and triangle-pointed hat of a fry cook. He learned to wait tables, run the cash register, wash dishes, and balance the books. He became an assistant manager, a store manager, an area manager, a district manager, and before he is 50, I am certain he will be a franchise owner. With hard work and a lot of bacon grease, my friend Brad genuinely has a wonderful career. He provides a marvelous life for his son, and Waffle House has given him a living and a salary he never thought possible – that's no joke either.

Brad told me how management works at Waffle House. The manager has to be able to do everything in the store. The manager is not a specialized, white collar, can't-get-dish-pan-hands kind of overseer. It is a hands-on, practical, flexible approach. And it's not just the manager. To keep a Waffle House up and running, there are few specialists. Everyone can do a little bit of everything – and that is the key. If you are going to survive in that business, you have to have adjustable settings. You have to be flexible.

Case in point: My family eats at Waffle House every Christmas Eve. It's as much a part of our tradition as Advent candles and eggnog. I cannot imagine celebrating Christmas without the smell of scrambled eggs in the air, the unintelligible banter of the fry cook in the background, Elvis singing "Blue Christmas" on the jukebox, and wonderful conversations with the restaurant staff and patrons (Have you ever had a conversation of any length with a Waffle House waitress or guest? I have never met anyone in said establishment who was not an absolutely extraordinary person.).

Anyway, this past year we were waiting on our meal to be served when our waitress horrendously crashed in the kitchen. She slipped on wet hash or something, and dropped like a sack of potatoes. I didn't see it. My son Bryce did.

He came over and said, "Hey, our waitress just wiped out."

I said, "Well, is she okay?"

He said, "I hope so. She was carrying my waffle."

His compassion was duly noted as one of the cooks took the fallen waitress' pad and pencil, and slid right to our table and carried on business as usual. The manager took a spot at the griddle. The kid cleaning in the back became the greeter. Everyone adjusted. There was flexibility: And that is the last serving in this series, "The Gospel According to Waffle House." It is about Flexibility.

As it should be, we return to Romans 15, words that have guided this series, verses 23-29:

*But now I have finished my work in these other regions, and after all these long years of waiting, I am eager to visit you. I am planning to go to Spain, and when I do, I will stop off in Rome. And after I have enjoyed your fellowship for a little while, you can provide for my journey. But before I come, I must go to Jerusalem to take a gift to the believers there. For you see, the believers in Macedonia and Achaia have eagerly taken up an offering for the poor among the believers in Jerusalem. They were glad to do this because they feel they owe a real debt to them. Since the Gentiles received the spiritual blessings of the Good News from the believers in Jerusalem, they feel the least they can do in return is to help them financially. As soon as I have delivered this money and completed this good deed of theirs, I will come to see you on my way to Spain. And I am sure that when I come, Christ will richly bless our time together* (NLT).

Paul had the best and long-held intentions to go to Rome and visit the church there. But "a funny thing happened on the way to the forum." Life happened. Paul was busy doing what he loved to do and doing what he was called to do. As a missionary traveler whose exploits would shame the hardiest Methodist circuit riding preacher of a generation ago, he was working his way toward Rome when somebody said, "Let's take up a love offering!" The new Gentile churches wanted to alleviate some of the financial strain for the Jerusalem church.

Remember, all the earliest Christians in Jerusalem were Jews. When they converted, they were more or less expelled from society and poverty exploded. Early Christians had to become self-sufficient. The Gentile churches wanted to help ease this burden, so a necessary bond was created between two very different ethnic groups; and this helped the church find its way in its earliest years. Paul would be the one who would now travel back to Jerusalem to take the offering. But then, another "funny thing happened on the way to the forum." Yes, he brought the offering back to Jerusalem, but then he got arrested by the authorities there for sedition, which led to a prolonged imprisonment of nearly three years. He had to appeal his case all the way to the Roman courts – all the way to Caesar himself.

So, finally, he got to Rome four years after he wrote these words to the Roman Christians, and he did not arrive with a community choir and a tent for a revival meeting. He arrived in chains, a prisoner. He was released, however, and may have in fact made it to Spain – the farthest reach of the civilized world at that time – we don't know for sure (I like to think that he made it there on his last expedition). But he landed in trouble again a few years later, and was deported back to Rome where he was eventually executed – he was beheaded – by orders of the infamous Nero.

There's a keen little proverb credited to Woody Allen that goes like this (I know you have heard it): "If you want to make God laugh, tell him your plans." Get busy organizing your life. Draft a game plan for everything from what time you will eat your meals to your projected career path. Tell yourself and those around you where you plan to be in 10 years, 20 years, or by retirement. Fix in your mind how you think life will go – and that sound you will hear in the distance will not be thunder. It will be God, splitting his sides and the heavens with uproarious hilarity.

Now, God's not going to throw a monkey wrench into your plans; I don't think he does things like that. He laughs because control is an illusion. Life twists and turns like a corkscrew. He knows. He's been around a while to observe such things. You can fight it – and never have a minute of peace ever again – or you can go with it.

Someone once came to me while in dire straits. It was a terrible situation, no doubt, but I observed that the greater pain was not the situation. It was the fact that the situation had gotten out of his "control." He said, "I just cannot take this; I will not accept it!"

Finally I asked, "But what choice do you have?"

Here is another spot I could just camp out with for a while. My God, the things we do to ourselves – not attempting to cope with our problems, no – but attempting to avoid reality; insisting with all rigidity to shape life in our image. But for our purposes today, let's make application to the church.

Churches organize – even this one. It is impossible to do otherwise. When two people get together to do something, even if it is to eat lunch, they organize for that purpose. Organization is not a dirty word. But there is, somewhere, a line that organizations (and churches) cross, where they transition from being a living thing made of living, breathing people, into a lifeless machine. They become a button-controlled, gear-driven contraption that runs on auto pilot and cannot change, adapt, or adjust. It's like the rise of the cyborgs: Organizations become less than human and actually degrade people rather than empower people.

If you don't believe me, consider this: You can work for, bleed for, and die for a people or person you love, and you will never be forgotten. If you work for, bleed for, and die for an organization, the ink won't be dry on your obituary before the machine rolls on without you.[13]

Think about it like this: In the mid-1980s the borough of Brooklyn in New York City found it necessary to repair and replace the Carroll Street Bridge. The Carroll Street Bridge was old. It had originally been built in 1889, so it was due some serious maintenance. It was determined that the bidding process would require two years, the construction of the bridge would require five more years, and the cost of construction would be $3.5 million. This was part and parcel to the process, but the 100-year anniversary of the building of the bridge was coming up. The city would like the bridge to be open by that date.

So Deputy Commissioner of Bridges Sam Schwartz decided to circumvent the process – a process that involved 35 individual steps and 6 different agencies – and fast-track the project. He got the money, the contracts, and the engineers on the job posthaste; and the bridge was finished in 11 months (not 7 years), at a savings of more than $1 million; and the bridge reopened for its centennial celebration! For his accomplishments,

Commissioner Schwartz was given an official reprimand from the city of New York and almost lost his job. Why? He had violated the organizational protocols. He had broken the rules. And rather than being lauded, he was punished.[14]

Churches are capable of the same! Much of our theology, structure, and practice started out well. It was organized for a good, even godly purpose, but it has devolved into command and control stiffness that is just plain lunacy! The situation on the ground has changed – and no one can admit it and go with it!

Just try to adjust the format or style of a church worship service.

Try to change a church's financial policies.

Attempt to replace the stained glass windows with all the little shiny brass tags from the donors who died 200 years ago.

Take a stab at streamlining the organizational structure.

Ask people to be flexible and pliant.

Before you know it, you might have a pitchfork-toting mob on your front steps. From my own experience, the biggest knock-down-drag-outs I have ever witnessed or participated in, are those that broke out when somebody wanted to change something in order to actually meet life where it had taken the group, and others couldn't adjust. Thus, the machine either ground the dissenters up, or the whole thing came to a screeching, grinding halt.

*At the risk of being grossly misunderstood, when the rules of the machine become more important than the people those rules are supposed to serve, the dysfunction has reached an incurable end. The condition is terminal. The gig is up. Quit, and move on to something else.*

"But Pastor, God is not a God of disorder." I've heard that verse quoted my whole life and have witnessed more chaos born of imposed "order" than anything that came out of allowing people just to be people! Such a quote, even a quote from the Bible, cannot serve as an excuse to manipulate, mistreat, oppress or otherwise stymie people's God-given spirit of freedom, vocation and expression. Such a quote cannot hold people, organizations, and processes hostage.

Heck, last time I went to a Waffle House it looked like chaos and confusion. Music was blaring, doors were slamming, bells were ringing, waitresses were shouting, pot and pans were clanging. You would be tempted to ask, "What is going on around here?" And the answer would come back: "Some real good stuff, that's what! We're rolling with the flow. We're getting it done. Our only rules are good food and good service. Everything else is up for grabs." And that is the kind of flexibility that will keep us on task doing what really matters, rather than keeping us trapped in the very system we created.

Since this has been a very personal series of talks, let me make it even more so here: Flexibility is going to be required of all of us in the days ahead. I know we are going to remain committed to our simple way of being church: "Worship God, Follow Jesus, and Serve Others." Beyond that, I don't know what might be required of us. We may have to move locations – no, we will most certainly move locations. We may have to share space with others. We may have to change the time of our Sunday morning gathering. We will have to be more intentional serving in the local community. We may have to explore new, different and exciting partnerships with others on the way. We may have to adjust our schedules. The content of our gatherings will adjust from time to time and so will its order – don't fight it – go with it![15]

Just imagine a tightrope in your mind – a wire that is pulled taut between two poles. One pole is people – we are here to love, welcome, serve, heal, befriend, and bear with people, inviting them to experience the kingdom of God in all its beautiful manifestations. The other pole is our simple, uncomplicated identity as Jesus-followers. We are absolutely committed to the words and ways of Christ – the "red letters" of the gospels. These are our two stationary points – the people we love and the Jesus who loves us.

Depending upon the situation and the context, we move all along that wire between the two, moving and adjusting the entire time. It's the only way, for if we don't move and adjust, we will fearfully cling to one pole or the other, or we'll lose our balance and fall off completely. Flexibility is simply that space between Christ and our calling. We have a lot of distance and play between the two – we must not be afraid to use it.

So no, I don't know what the future holds, but I know this: The challenges we will face in our community, in our vocation, and even within our individual lives will not stick with the script. Sure, we can have all these planning meetings in the back rooms of an office building or at some far away retreat, preparing for each and every contingency. But, we don't know each and every contingency. Like Paul, we may think we will be in Rome next week and on to the Spanish coast by spring time. No! You will be surprised – stunned – by what develops. The pre-drafted policy and operational models that may have worked in the controlled, sterile environment of the board room, will not always work in the actual situation where life happens.

I'll share a final example where I personally learned this lesson of flexibility: I first moved to Walton County, Florida in the winter of 2004-2005 to become the Executive Director of the local Habitat for Humanity affiliate. I was never – never – going to lead a congregation again; and I said as much – never. God laughed. I am eternally grateful to Buz and Susan Livingston and Rena Anderson for the invitation to move into this community, an act that has changed my life in a most profound way, a way I never saw coming. But enough of that.

Shortly after moving here, Hurricane Katrina hit the Gulf Coast. Our affiliate and community felt compelled to assist the people of Pearlington, Mississippi, a small village that looked like ground zero of a nuclear explosion. I remember seeing the high water mark at the local elementary school; it was a foot above the basketball goals in the gymnasium. People like the Livingtons, Jay Gates, Penny Benson, Russell Meade, Buster Woodruff, and many others threw themselves into the work, and the Habitat affiliate served as the fiscal agent for the efforts.

We jumped in with what we thought was the best laid plan possible. It was a good plan, an excellent plan. But within ten days of being in Mississippi, our fine-tuned plan and machinery had passed through a meat grinder. On paper, it was perfect! On the ground, it turned into compost, and I had a hard time adjusting. I'd say things like:

> *"It shouldn't be this hard."*
> *"How can a situation be so difficult?"*
> *"Why won't people cooperate?"*

I had drafted this wonderful plan to help people – and was responsible for its execution – and I just could not accept the fact that my plan needed to change. *See, I was more committed to my strategy than finding a workable solution.*

This changed when I encountered a man we nicknamed, "Captain Gumbo." He said his

house on the Pearl River had been washed
away. We discovered later that this was not
true. He was trying to get a new house out of
us, for he had never lived on dry ground. He
lived on a boat, and saw our generous relief
efforts as a means of "coming ashore." We
didn't know this until the building materials
had already been delivered to his little piece of
land. When we went to repossess our building
materials, Captain Gumbo was sitting on top
of this great stack of lumber and shingles with
a pistol on each hip and a sawed-off shotgun.
Then, finally, I got it. This plan probably
needs to be adjusted.

But I wasn't the only one suffering from
rigidity. In the aftermath of Hurricane Katrina
I had the opportunity to work with some of
the most talented people on the Gulf Coast:
Influential, brilliant individuals, but they all,
like me, seemed more committed to their plan
than to people. The architects wanted their
designs patented and protected. Elected
officials wanted to ensure votes for the next
primary. Donors wanted recognition, a brass
plate attached to anything and everything they
financed. Large non-profits wanted to tightly
control everything that was going on and
guard their brand identity. Reporters wanted
the next tear-jerking story. Meanwhile, the

people of Pearlington, Mississippi just wanted a roof over their heads. As a whole, with all these collective resources and motivations, we never quite got around to completing that most important thing.

I might have needed to face a gun-wielding Cajun to understand, but I got it. And I don't ever want to have to admit again, that inflexibility and rigidity got in the way of what was most important. Let none of us ever have to admit that here.

Ω Ω Ω

Dear God, help us to bend to life's winds and to your will. Help us to focus on what is really important and on what will give all of us your life. Free us from inflexibility, and grant us the gift of faith that we might trust in you. In Christ we pray, Amen.

# AS YOU LEAVE THE TABLE...

Well, there you have it, what I hope has been a feast worthy of feeding your heart and soul. As you push yourself away from the table, I hope you have a satisfied feeling of fullness; that peculiar contentment that comes from good food "hitting the spot." But whatever you do with what you have read, now is not the time to head over to the couch and collapse into a post-meal coma. As full as you may be, resist the temptation to fall asleep with it. Food is for the purpose of energy and empowerment, not stagnation.

I suppose I learned this lesson in my maternal grandmother's kitchen, a woman whose culinary and hospitality skills would have disgraced the heartiest Waffle House operation. Grandmother, and everyone called her "Grandmother," lived her entire life on a farm. First, it was cotton, then it was soybean, and finally it was cows and chickens. I spent the summers of my youth on that farm, working in my uncle's chicken houses, chasing stray cows, and bailing and stacking hay. The work demanded boundless stamina, and the days started early and ran late. It took a great deal of fuel to work that hard and that long. But my grandmother, the master that she was, could meet the demands.

She cooked for everyone who was working: My uncle and aunt, several of the grandchildren, the hired help, and sometimes the neighbors. On any given summer day, you could gather around her big oak table and find it running over with everything battered, greased, and iron-skillet fried. Chicken, gravy, biscuits, squash, coconut pie, mashed potatoes, sweet tea, cornbread – all the things that doctors now say will kill you. It was wonderful.

A man or a woman could eat like that for lunch, rest a few minutes in the shade of the front yard, and then have the energy to work the rest of the day. And guess what? Nobody on the farm was obese, had high cholesterol, high blood pressure, or had cardiac issues or diabetes. Nobody. Why? Because when you put your hand to the work that must be done, you can eat whatever you want and as much as you want without harming yourself. You need it, and you burn it up.

My grandmother is gone now, and most of the family farm has been sold as well. Mass-produced little houses and subdivisions sit on the land that used to produce cotton or graze cows. Consequently, no one in my family works as hard as they used to either. Many of us never even leave the comfort of air conditioning to make a living. The problem is that a few of us still eat like we're working on the farm. The result is obesity, high cholesterol, high blood pressure, open heart surgery, diabetes, and all the other afflictions of a softer society. We're simply not working off the calories.

Christians, likewise, are often overeaters. No, not necessarily at meal time, though you will find more than one rotund Bible-thumper in front of you at the Sunday buffet (or sitting next to you at Waffle House). We have an eating disorder when it comes to getting our "spiritual food."

Give me the richest music.

Feed me with good preaching.

Fill my cavernous belly.

Pass the bread and the wine.

Before you know it we are so plump and

drunk we can't get off the pew to help our neighbors. We become "pew potatoes," as greasy as any hash brown, that sit, feast, and nap, but refuse to get up and "work it off" in the fields of God's farm. So we are fat, slow, and unfit.

There are more than 300,000 churches in the United States. Americans give $93 billion dollars a year to houses of worship, but then we spend eighty-five cents out of every dollar on ourselves. Further, only two cents out of every dollar put in the offering plate ever makes it out of the country. We mow down acres of forests and spill gallons of ink, buying $5 billion of Christian books, studies, and other products every year, just to aid our personal spiritual growth. To lament that you can't get spiritually "fed" is like complaining of starvation while standing in line at the all-you-can-eat Chinese buffet.

The challenge before us is not a lack of information; it is the lack of implementation. We must rise from mealtime and take the hundreds of sermons and songs; the countless books (just like this one) and Bible studies; and the millions of Christian words that land on our ears week after week and year after year, and put them into action in our lives, our churches, and our communities. We must take the multitude baskets of broken bread, the jars of flowing wine, the bountiful table spread before us each day like a Southern feast, and empowered by it, do the work God has called each of us to do.

For me, God's calling is characterized by what you have read about on these pages: Welcoming all people to find their identity in the simple, gracious way of Jesus. But if this calling is only expressed with words, only pages on paper or a digital screen, it means very little. It has to be "worked" out.

Thankfully, I journey with a group of people attempting to do exactly that. I pray you are privileged to have the same, because while there comes an end to all of our words, there will never be an end to our work.

May we be found ready, for we have been well fed for the task at hand.

# ABOUT THE AUTHOR

Ronnie McBrayer was born and raised in the foothills of the North Georgia Mountains, and claims he barely survived the fire-and-brimstone churches located there. Shaped by this experience, Ronnie has spent his lifetime preaching and protesting; loving and leaving; resisting and returning to faith – faith in Jesus. With this contagious trust in Christ, a schoolboy wit, and his applauded story-telling style, Ronnie invites his readers and listeners to reflect, laugh, face the unexpected, and to be changed by the grace of God.

He leads *A Simple Faith* in Santa Rosa Beach, Florida and is the author of multiple publications including *Leaving Religion, Following Jesus*; *The Jesus Tribe*; and *How Far is Heaven?* Additionally, McBrayer's weekly newspaper and internet column, "Keeping the Faith," is nationally syndicated with a circulation of more than six million readers. And he can be found every Christmas Eve eating at a local Waffle House.

For more information about the author, or if you are interested in Ronnie speaking to your group or congregation, please visit his website at www.ronniemcbrayer.me.

## Ω Ω Ω

## Other Titles by Ronnie McBrayer

*But God Meant It for Good: Lessons From the Life of Joseph*

*Leaving Religion, Following Jesus*

*Keeping the Faith, Volume 1*

*Keeping the Faith, Volume 2*

*The Jesus Tribe: Following Christ in the Land of the Empire*

*How Far Is Heaven?: Rediscovering the Kingdom of God in the Here and Now*

# ENDNOTES

*This is a portion of T.S. Eliot's poem, *Four Quartets*, first published in 1943.

[1] Lewis Grizzard, "Gnawing Problem Is Solved," *The Atlanta Journal*, August 7, 1992.

[2] This quote is directly from the Waffle House website, www.wafflehouse.com.

[3] *The Little Shop of Horrors*, Directed by Roger Corman, Written by Charles B. Griffith, 1960.

[4] Rodney Clapp, *A Peculiar People*, IVP Academic, 1996, 114-119.

[5] This is a favorite saying of Rev. Jether Cochran.

[6] See Jamie Wright's blog post, "Jesus or Zoloft?" at www.theveryworstmissionary.com/2013/01/jesus-or-zoloft.html.

[7] This quote is directly from the Waffle House website, www.wafflehouse.com.

[8]Download the free e-book, *Renew 52* at: www.luthersem.edu/vcp/renew52/default.aspx.

[9]Frederick Buechner, *Listening to Your Life*, Harper SanFrancisco, 205-206.

[10]An informative article on the Waffle House Disaster Index is Valerie Bauerlein's "How to Measure a Storm's Fury One Breakfast at a Time," in *The Wall Street Journal*, September 1, 2011.

[11]Panos Kouvelis, PhD, in "Disaster Management Allows Companies to Get Ahead of the Game," online at http://www.newswise.com/articles/disaster -management-allows-companies-to-get-ahead-of-the-game.

[12]This prayer is adapted from Thomas Merton.

[13]This is a loose summary of a phrase often quoted by Dr. Bill Leonard, Wake Forest School of Divinity.

[14]James Emery White and Leighton Ford, *Rethinking the Church: A Challenge to Creative Redesign in an Age of Transition*, Baker, 116-117.

[15]Ironically (or providentially), within months almost every transition mentioned in this paragraph came to fruition.

25914181R00065

Made in the USA
Charleston, SC
18 January 2014